I Wonder Why

Fish Grew Legs

and Other Questions About Prehistory

Jackie Gaff

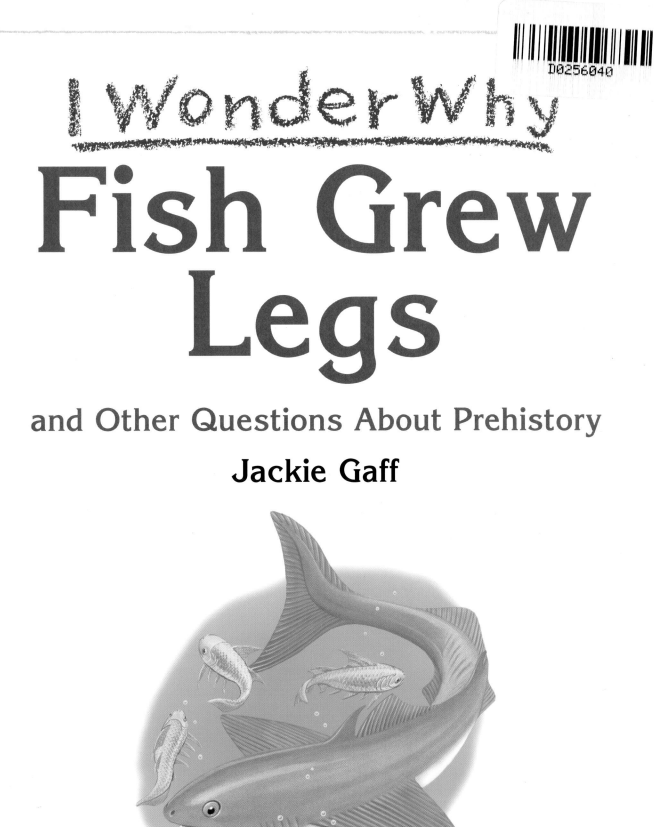

KING*f*ISHER

KINGFISHER
Kingfisher Publications Plc,
New Penderel House,
283-288 High Holborn,
London WC1V 7HZ
www.kingfisherpub.com

First published by Kingfisher Publications Plc 2001
10 9 8 7 6 5 4 3 2 1

ITR/0401/TIM/RNB/MA128

A CIP catalogue record for this book
is available from the British Library

ISBN 0 7534 0553 9

Series designer: David West Children's Books
Author: Jackie Gaff
Consultant: Steve Parker
Illustrations: James Field (SGA) 12, 14–15, 16–17,
18–19, 20–21, 22–23, 24–25, 26–27; Andrew
Harland (SGA) 7b, 10–11; Mike Lacey (SGA) 4–5,
29, 30–31; Sarah Smith (SGA) 6–7t, 7b, 8t, 9b, 13;
Stephen Sweet (SGA) 4t, 5b; Ross Watton (SGA) 6b,
8b, 8-9t, 28; Peter Wilks (SGA) all cartoons.

Printed in China

CONTENTS

What is prehistory?

Prehistory is the time before people began to record in writing the things that happened to them and in the world around them. It is the story of Earth from its birth to the invention of writing, about 5,500 years ago.

● The first proper writing system was invented by people called the Sumerians, who lived in the area we now call the Middle East.

● In this book, mya is short for 'million years ago'.

● Earth formed about 4,600 mya, from a cloud of dust and gas spinning around the Sun.

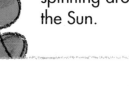

• Before the scientific study of fossils began in the late 1700s, some people thought fossils were real animals that had been turned into stone by hot sunlight.

How do we know about prehistoric life?

People who study prehistoric life work like detectives, slowly piecing clues together from fossils – the stony remains of animals and plants that died millions of years ago.

• Most fossils formed after a dead plant or animal sank to the bottom of a river, lake or sea, and was covered by layers of sand or mud.

• Over millions of years, the sand and mud hardened into rock, with the animal or plant buried inside as a stony fossil.

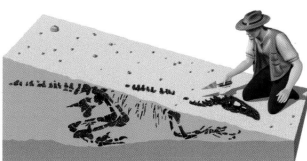

5

When did life on Earth begin?

Earth was a boiling hot mass of rock at first. Millions of years passed before its surface cooled down enough for life to survive. The first living things may have appeared as long as 4,000 mya, but so far scientists have not found fossils to prove this. The earliest-known fossils belong to microscopically tiny bacteria which lived in the oceans about 3,500 mya.

● The first many-celled creatures looked a bit like worms, jellyfish and sea anemones. Their bodies were soft and squishy, without bones or shells.

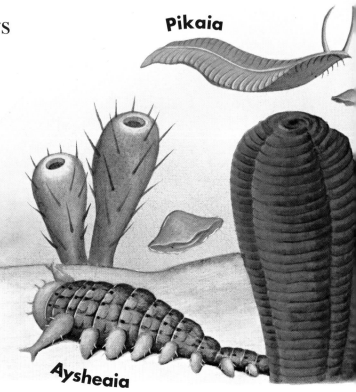

Pikaia

Aysheaia

● In some places the bacteria clustered together into mat-like sheets, which built up into mounds called stromatolites. Over time, the stromatolites became fossils.

Stromatolites

What is evolution?

Evolution is what scientists call the gradual change of one kind of living thing into another. It happens very, very slowly. The first bacteria were tiny single cells. It took more than 2,500 million years for the earliest-known larger creatures, with bodies made up of many cells, to evolve.

Eldonia

Hallucigenia

• Dickinsonia was as wide as a swimming ring – it measured 60 centimetres across.

What is extinction?

Not all living things carry on evolving. Sometimes, a particular kind of animal or plant dies out and disappears from Earth completely. This is extinction.

Trilobite

• Trilobites evolved at least 600 mya, and became extinct about 240 mya. They were among the first animals to have eyes, and they were some of the earliest to have bodies protected by a tough shell-like exoskeleton.

When did fish appear in the oceans?

Sacabambaspis

When fish evolved about 500 mya, they were the first animals to have proper backbones. They had no jaws or fins, however, and looked rather like modern-day tadpoles.

● With no jaws for biting or chewing, early fish like Arandaspis fed by hoovering up tiny creatures from the seabed.

Climatius

Cladoselache

Cheirolepis

● Dunkleosteus was a whopping six metres long, but it wasn't a shark. This scary monster belonged to a group called the armoured fish, because of the bony plates that protected their heads from attackers' teeth.

Dunkleosteus

Were sharks around in prehistoric times?

They certainly were – sharks were cruising the oceans by about 400 mya. They were among the earliest of the backboned animals to develop jaws and hard teeth, and they were just as ferocious as today's sharks!

● You wouldn't want to go swimming with Stethacanthus. The top of this early shark's weird T-shaped fin was covered in teethlike bristles, and so was its head.

What were the sea scorpions?

The sea scorpions were fierce hunters with barbed claws for snatching up their food. They lived at the same time as the early sharks and grew to two metres long. They did not have a backbone. Instead, their bodies were covered by a shell-like exoskeleton.

Pterygotus

When did plants get a foothold on land?

Plants were successful on land before animals, and the earliest-known fossils of a land plant date back to about 420 mya. Scientists call the plant Cooksonia, and it was tiny – about as tall as your little finger.

● Although Cooksonia had a stem, it didn't have leaves, flowers or proper roots.

Why were prehistoric plants important?

The arrival of land plants meant that there was enough food around for land animals to evolve too. Among the first to eat up their greens were tiny mites, and insects such as springtails.

Protocarus

Diplopodan

● All animals need oxygen to survive. Because plants use the Sun's energy to turn carbon dioxide into oxygen, they helped to bump up the air's oxygen levels.

● Once plant-eating land animals were around, meat-eaters evolved to munch on them.

Why did fish pop their heads above water?

Most fish take oxygen from the water through their gills. But after land plants appeared, something weird happened – some kinds of fish developed lungs for breathing air. Scientists call them lungfish, and think they evolved because there wasn't enough oxygen in the shallow rivers and lakes where they lived.

Mesaraneus

● The weather became much warmer at the time that lungfish evolved. Water evaporated and turned into gas, making lakes and rivers shallower, with less oxygen.

Eusthenopteron

Why did fish grow legs?

Some fish didn't just grow lungs, their fins became legs and they evolved into land animals! The earliest four-legged animals, Acanthostega and Ichthyostega, appeared about 370 mya. They spent most of their time in the water, but they could crawl about on land.

● Acanthostega and Ichthyostega were ancestors of the amphibians – animals that can live on land, but which lay their eggs in water.

Ichthyostega

● Diplocaulus was a bizarre early amphibian with a boomerang-shaped head. It lived mainly underwater, where its head worked like a submarine's hydrofoils.

Acanthostega

● Gigantic plants called clubmosses towered above warm, boggy swamps during the age of coal. Some grew to 40 metres – as high as a 15-storey block of flats!

Where did coal come from?

Most of the coal we burn today was formed from the remains of the prehistoric forests that covered the land between 355 and 290 mya. This period of time is called the age of coal.

Meganeura

Protarthrolycosa

Palaeopodiulus

Which insect was as big as a bird?

Meganeura was a huge dragonfly which flitted through the swampy forests of the age of coal. Its wings measured a massive 60 centimetres across.

● Insects such as dragonflies were the first flying animals.

When did reptiles appear?

Reptiles were a new group of animals which evolved from amphibians towards the end of the age of coal. Reptiles such as Hylonomus were the first four-legged animals to live in dry places where there was little water.

Hylonomus

● Reptiles have dry scaly skin, and their eggs don't dry out because each egg is protected by a leathery shell.

● Amphibian eggs have no shells, so they have to be laid in water to stop them drying out.

Which animals grew sails?

It isn't hard to work out how sailbacks like Dimetrodon got their name! Their sail-like fin probably worked rather like a solar panel, soaking up the Sun's heat.

Dimetrodon

● The sailbacks were reptiles, and reptiles are sunbathers. They love the Sun because they are cold-blooded – they cannot keep their blood warm without the Sun's heat.

Cynognathus

Which were the first furry animals?

Hair helps to keep animals warm, so most warm-blooded animals have furry or feathery coats. Scientists think the first warm-blooded furry animals were a type of reptile called the cynodonts, which evolved about 250 mya.

What were the ruling reptiles?

The ruling reptiles were the ancestors of the dinosaurs. Earlier reptiles had walked on all fours, but by 240 mya, ruling reptiles such as Euparkeria were able to scurry along on two back legs – especially when chasing a tasty meal!

Euparkeria

● One of the ways scientists find out what dinosaurs ate is by studying stony fossils of dino-droppings – it's a good thing fossils aren't smelly!

Dryosaurus

Stegosaurus

Camptosaurus

Compsognathus

● Fossils of more than 800 kinds of dinosaur have been found and named, but scientists think there may have been at least twice as many.

How long did dinosaurs rule the land?

The earliest-known dinosaurs appeared about 230 mya, and the last ones died out about 65 mya. So dinosaurs were around for a mind-boggling 165 million years!

- Brachiosaurus was tall enough to munch at the top of the highest trees.

Brachiosaurus

- All sorts of different dinosaurs evolved during their 165 million years on Earth, from the turkey-sized meat-eater Compsognathus, to the gigantic plant-eater Brachiosaurus.

Allosaurus

Did dinosaurs rule the skies?

The dinosaurs did not have wings for flying. Other kinds of reptile called pterosaurs ruled the skies in dinosaur times. Pterosaurs came in all shapes and sizes, but they all had wings. Quetzalcoatlus was the biggest – its 12-metre wingspan made it the size of a small aircraft.

● Pterodaustro probably used its strange bristly teeth like a sieve, to strain tiny sea creatures from the water.

Quetzalcoatlus

● Scientists have found fossils that show some pterosaurs had furry bodies, like modern-day bats.

Rhamphorhynchus

Peloneustes

● Like land reptiles, the sea reptiles breathed air. Most of them had to return to land to lay their eggs.

Elasmosaurus

● Pterosaurs' wings were leathery flaps of skin which hung from one enormously long finger on each hand.

Pterodactylus

Did dinosaurs rule the seas?

Dinosaurs were land animals, and other reptiles ruled the seas in dinosaur times. Some of these sea reptiles looked rather like dinosaurs, though – Elasmosaurus had a long neck, just like Brachiosaurus.

Pterodaustro

● At over 15 metres from nose to tail, Liopleurodon was as long as a bus!

Ichthyosaurus

Liopleurodon

● Ichthyosaurus never had to flop about on dry land. Instead of laying eggs, it gave birth to live baby Ichthyosauruses – underwater.

Where did birds come from?

Dinosaurs may not have been able to fly, but scientists think that birds evolved from dinosaurs, and not from pterosaurs. The earliest-known feathered flyer was Archaeopteryx. It lived over 145 mya and scientists think it was a dinobird – half-dinosaur and half-bird.

Archaeopteryx

● Caudipteryx was another feathered dinobird, but it couldn't fly – its wings were too small.

● The duckbilled dinosaurs were gentle plant-eaters that came along after flowering plants appeared.

Edmontosaurus

When did the first flowers bloom?

Flowering plants didn't appear until about 140 mya, so only the later kinds of dinosaur would have seen and smelled them. Two of the earliest trees to blossom and fruit were magnolias and figs.

● Fossil-hunters have found part of a meat-eating dinosaur bigger than Tyrannosaurus. They've called it Giganotosaurus, which means 'giant southern lizard'.

Why was Tyrannosaurus king of the dinosaurs?

Tyrannosaurus

Imagine a giant with teeth as long as your hands and a mouth that's big enough to swallow you whole – that was Tyrannosaurus. It was one of the largest meat-eating land animals the world has ever known, and that's why it is called king of the dinosaurs.

● Tyrannosaurus was among the last kinds of dinosaur to evolve, fewer than 70 mya. Its name means 'tyrant lizard' (a tyrant is a cruel ruler).

Were mammals around in dinosaur times?

The first mammals had probably evolved from cynodonts by about 220 mya, a few million years after the first dinosaurs appeared. The earliest mammals were furry insect-eaters, not much bigger than modern-day mice.

Megazostrodon

Kamptobaator

Taeniolabis

Ptilodus

Zalambdalestes

● Megazostrodon could have sat on your hand – from its nose to the tip of its tail it only measured 12 centimetres.

●One of the special things about mammals is that mothers make milk in their bodies for their babies to feed on.

● The babies of most of the mammals living today develop in their mother's womb. They aren't born until they're big enough to survive in the outside world.

Which babies lived in their mother's pocket?

Early mammals laid eggs, as their ancestors the reptiles had done. Over time though, other mammals evolved. These gave birth to their babies, instead of hatching them from eggs. Marsupials first appeared about 100 mya. Marsupials are mammals whose newborn babies grow up in a pocket-like pouch on their mother's tummy.

Deltatheridium

● Newborn marsupials are no bigger than a jelly baby! They live in their mother's pouch until they are able to find their own food outside the pouch.

How do we know the dinosaurs died out?

Fossil-hunters haven't found anything to show that even a single lonely dinosaur has been alive during the past 65 million years – no fossil dinosaur bones, no fossil dinosaur footprints, nothing. All of the dinosaurs vanished 65 mya, along with all the pterosaurs and most of the sea reptiles.

Scientists haven't found dinosaur fossils in rocks that formed after 65 mya.

● Well over half of all the different kinds of animal on Earth became extinct 65 mya. No large animals seem to have survived beyond this time.

● We cannot be sure that it was the space rock that changed Earth's weather and killed off the dinosaurs. Some scientists think that exploding volcanoes sent up dust clouds to block out the Sun.

What killed the dinosaurs?

Many scientists think that the dinosaurs were wiped out after a city-sized chunk of space rock crashed into the Earth 65 mya. The impact was like tens of thousands of bombs exploding. Huge waves swept across the oceans and the land. Vast clouds of dust flew up into the sky, blotting out the Sun and plummeting Earth into icy darkness.

● Plants cannot grow without sunlight, so the big plant-eating animals died of cold and hunger first, and then the big meat-eaters.

● Some people used to think that the dinosaurs died out because the mammals ate all their eggs!

● No one knows for sure why some animals survived and others didn't. Perhaps it was because they were small enough to hide in burrows.

Which animals took over from the dinosaurs?

With no meat-eating dinosaurs around to hunt them, more and more new kinds of mammal began to evolve. Most were land animals, but some took to the air and others to the seas.

Icaronycteris

● Bats are flying mammals. One of the earliest-known bats was Icaronycteris, which appeared about 54 mya.

Smilodectes

Uintatherium

Hoplophoneus

Stylinodon

● Anancus had a hard time holding up its head. This early elephant's huge tusks were almost as long as the rest of its body.

● Whales are sea mammals which evolved at about the same time as bats. The earliest-known whale, Pakicetus, looked more like an otter than the whales of today.

Pakicetus

When were elephants as small as pigs?

Moeritherium

Elephants went through all sorts of weird and wonderful stages before they evolved into the animals we know today. When Moeritherium appeared about 40 mya, it was one of the earliest elephants – and only 60 centimetres high!

● When horses appeared about 50 mya, they were tiny, too. Hyracotherium had toes instead of hooves, and was cat-sized – about 20 centimetres high.

Indricotherium

Brontotherium

Protocerus

Which cats had dagger-sized teeth?

Hoplophoneus

The sabre-toothed cats were named because of their massive fangs. These weren't used for eating, but for stabbing and killing their victims!

Who was Lucy?

Around 4.5 mya, some new mammals appeared on the scene – the earliest human-like creatures. They have scientific names such as Australopithecus, which means 'southern ape'. It's a bit of a mouthful, though, so it's easier to use nick-names, such as Lucy.

● Lucy's fossilized skeleton was found in Africa in 1974. She was named after a Beatles' song, 'Lucy in the sky with diamonds', which was playing on the fossil-hunters' radio at the time.

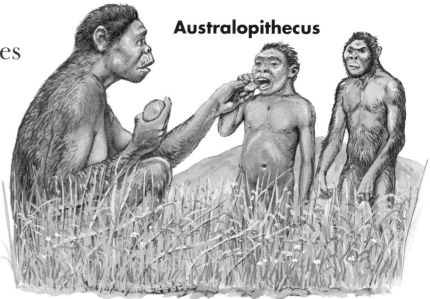

Australopithecus

Homo habilis

When did humans get handy?

Homo habilis means 'handy human', and these human ancestors were named because they were probably the first to use tools. They lived about two mya, and their tools were simple stone pebbles.

Who were the first explorers?

Although all early humans evolved in Africa, Homo erectus, who appeared about 1.9 mya, were very adventurous people. They were the first to head north out of Africa and explore Asia and Europe.

Homo erectus

● Homo erectus means 'upright human'.

● Homo sapiens were the first Australians. They sailed there from southeast Asia more than 50,000 years ago.

Who were the wise humans?

Modern humans are clever, which is why our scientific name is Homo sapiens, meaning 'wise human'. Our closest ancestors, the first Homo sapiens, evolved in Africa almost 200,000 years ago.

Homo sapiens

What were the Ice Ages?

The Ice Ages were long periods of time when it was so cold that snow and ice spread down from the North Pole to cover vast areas of Europe, Asia and North America. The Ice Ages began about 2 mya, and the last one melted away after the weather began warming up again about 12,000 years ago.

● Mammoths lived in northern lands, where their woolly coats kept them warm. The climate got too hot for them after the last Ice Age ended, and they became extinct.

Did Ice Age people live in caves?

They did if they could find one, but they also built huts from tree branches, or from mammoth bones and tusks covered in animal skins.

• The first crops were wheat and barley, and the first farm animals were goats and sheep.

• Some of the earliest-known huts were built about 400,000 years ago, by Homo erectus at a place called Terra Amata, on the southern French coast.

Who were the first farmers?

Farming began about 10,000 years ago, when people in the Middle East began saving the seeds of wild plants to sow as their own crops. Growing their own food meant that farmers could stay in the same place all year round. They built villages, which grew into towns, and then into cities. Prehistory was over and, with the invention of writing, modern human history had begun.

Index